CRA
CELEBRITY CODE

The Ultimate Leverage for
Entrepreneurs and Business Professionals
to Increase Leads, Referrals and Sales WITHOUT
Spending a Dime on Advertising

Rey Perez

ISBN: 978-1-65766-761-7

Disclaimer and Terms of Use: The Author and Publisher has strived to be as accurate and complete as possible in the creation of this book, notwithstanding the fact that they do not warrant or represent at any time that the contents within are accurate due to the rapidly changing nature of the internet. While all attempts have been made to verify information provided in this publication, the Author and the Publisher assume no responsibility for errors, omissions, or contrary interpretation of the subject matter herein. Any perceived slights of specific persons, peoples, or organizations are unintentional. In practical advice books, like anything else in life, there are no guarantees of income made. Readers are cautioned to rely on their own judgment about their individual circumstances to act accordingly. This book is not intended for use as a source of legal, business, accounting or financial advice. All readers are advised to seek the services of competent professionals in legal, business, accounting, and finance field.

For information on quantity sales: Special discounts are available on quantity purchases for corporations, associations, U.S. trade bookstores, wholesalers and independent booksellers. For details, contact Rey Perez at reyperez@iampyourbrand.com

Authority Positioning Publishing Strategy by Mike Saunders, MBA
https://www.AuthorityPositioningCoach.com

Rey Perez is Founder & CEO of Multimedia Marketing & Event Promotions Company, AMP Productions. Rey is a National Speaker, Successful Entrepreneur, Talk Show Host, Elite Business Coach and Philanthropist who leads Mastermind Groups, Marketing Seminars and Socially Infused-Networking Events across the country. He has shared the stage and worked with some of the biggest industry icons such as Les Brown, Jack Canfield, Bob Proctor, Kevin Harrington, Forbes Riley and many more.

Leveraging over 15 years of sales and marketing experience, Rey and his team create world-class celebrity brands for top entrepreneurs and professionals who want to dominate their niche or industry.

Rey entered the field of branding and marketing after spending years in promoting high-touch VIP events in Miami's nightlife scene. He saw how beneficial it was to engage consumers through photography and video production, and as we moved more into the digital age, the internet sped up the ability for more effective marketing. His goal with clients is to look into the visual and marketing strategy within their brand and capitalize on their unique selling proposition (USP). The riches are truly in the niches. Therefore, he looks at what clients are great at and why they are great at it. This allows him to make his clients a superstar brand.

The clients he typically serves include speakers, coaches, authors, consultants, trainers, small business owners, and entrepreneurs who are personality-driven and the face of their business. Rey's greatest success is to hear the stories of his clients breaking into 6-figures, multiple 6-figures, and even the 7-figure sales range.

Connect with Rey Perez: www.ReyPerez360.com

WELCOME!

I want to start by thanking you for giving me the opportunity to tell my story. This book touches upon the guiding principles that have helped me grow my business significantly, and my hope is that after reading, you are able to implement these principles.

This book is written in a unique way to immerse yourself in the content through a conversational writing style as if I am speaking straight to you.

You will also find that you will learn more easily from this book, not only because of the flow of the content, but there is also an integrated Workbook which allows you to implement your learning!

My hope is that you come away from this experience with a dramatic shift in your outlook on both your personal and professional life!

Let's get started!

Rey

TABLE OF CONTENTS

Foreword

As a Transformational Speaker, Catalyst for Change and a Messenger of Hope, I align and resonate with powerful leaders. Rey Perez is one of those leaders. As the #1 Global Branding Expert, he teaches you how to build better quality relationships faster, leverage personal branding so that you easily create trust and sell more!

Let me ask you something, Why is the "Air Jordan" the most popular Nike of all time? Why do fragrance brands fight and scratch to get influencers like J-Lo to be the face of the brand? Because people want to be like Celebrities. Period.

Imagine what would it be like if you were the Celebrity in your industry, do you think it would optimize your brand? I think so too!

Rey Perez has a God-given talent which is to connect with you and pull the greatness out and turn it into a digital presence so the world can see it and can be attracted to you! This will build raving fans; and if you have raving fans, then you have promoters of you, your message, your service, and you impact more people in the world!

I want to tell you something, you have something special, you have greatness within you! This book Rey published, "Cracking the Celebrity Code", will teach you how to achieve this, and more!

Les Brown

The Entrepreneur's Agency

The Entrepreneur's Agency was something we came up with after it had already been in business for about 15 years, after owning my own production company, and after having several different events for entrepreneurs and business owners. All of our events are "done-for-you" style events; entrepreneurs come to our studio in Miami, Florida, and we will either build out their brand, build out their videos, or build out their website. Everything we do focuses on done-for-you services.

The really exciting part is that my entire team is built from other entrepreneurs that have their own area of expertise in all of these different marketing fields. So, for example, some have expertise in branding, marketing, web development, app development, social media, photography, and video production. These are all the different services that entrepreneurs like me need in their business.

After 15 years of using every single service that is out there, I just thought to myself, "What if I pulled everything together and was the one-stop-shop **for** entrepreneurs **by** entrepreneurs?" And that's what we refer to as The Entrepreneur's Agency because it's for entrepreneurs, by entrepreneurs and provides every single service that they will need to grow, launch, and build a successful business.

The Benefit of Being Our Own Client

We've tested, we've tweaked, we've invested a tremendous amount of money, and we've seen the results. Then, it became a service that we could offer to other entrepreneurs because we use it on a daily basis, and it works for us. And that's one of the most beautiful parts about my job, my business, and what I call my family of entrepreneurs because we're not just providing value, we're providing results. And for me, that's one of the most important things that entrepreneurs nowadays really need to have.

THE POWER OF "DONE FOR YOU"

The reality is this: I've realized that time is the most valuable thing we have. In the words of the famous Jim Rohn: "You can get more money, but you can't get more time." And I've realized that only providing a high-value quality service at a good price point is not enough nowadays.

Entrepreneurs really want and need a good quality service at a good price point, but in a very fast turnaround time. The time it takes to receive the deliverables, you must consider how much more revenue you could have been producing, in that time. Usually, with branding and marketing, all the different services that we provide, take a decent amount of time. It could take up to several weeks or even several months to deliver!

Being a system-oriented person and the way that my mind works, it's always about creating systems, processes and automations, that allow you to produce more in a shorter amount of time, which is how I run my entire business.

So everything that we deliver is not only done for you services, it's not only high quality at a good price point, but we do it in a turnaround time that practically doesn't exist anywhere else on the planet. I feel very confident to be able to say that because, for example, at our Brand in 2 Days event, we literally will build someone's personal brand from head to toe with copywriting, photography, graphic design, social media, web presence, and marketing strategies in 48 hours. Done for you. Ready to rock and roll.

We have another event called OnScreen in 2 Days. This is all about video. So people who want to have a video presence, who want to learn how to use video in their marketing in 48 hours, we not only will teach them multiple different strategies of how to be effective with their video through social media, their web presence and all of that, but also produce professionally edited videos for them AND we'll shoot all the videos for them within 48 hours.

Some of them are delivered within those 48 hours, and then some will come within the next couple days as well. But still, most companies don't even have a strategy session and game plan to tell their team what they have to do within 48 hours.

We actually deliver it for our clients.

We have many other events like this that are all based around producing high-quality results through marketing, branding, production, all these different media at a great price point in a fast turnaround time. And again, it doesn't exist anywhere else on the planet.

DONE WITH YOU

So even though it is 100% done for you, the work is actually done WITH you. You are involved in the entire process. You're confirming that it's exactly the way that you want it to be and you have your revisions, and you can edit and change things. You are involved 100% of the time so that you're not only getting the results that you're looking for and the outcome that you want, but you're also learning on how to leverage it, which is really valuable. Not many marketing companies that I'm aware of deliver for you a marketing action plan along with the fast turnaround.

We call this our Personal Brand Marketing Action Plan (MAP), and this is probably the most valuable part of what we do in our events because we will give you a step-by-step plan with videos and a written-out checklist of what to do with the products that we're creating for you. This is very important because you may have a great piece of branding with a great video (you did an awesome job. It looks beautiful) but the question is, what do you do with it? What's the marketing strategy?

So for our Marketing Action Plan (MAP), at each of our events, we'll actually give the business owner and their team (some of them bring their assistants or their marketing person with them) a step-by-step guide on how to implement strategies get more leads, referrals, and sales by leveraging the power of your personal brand.

More Than Just Tangible Branding – You Will AMP Up Your Internal Confidence in YOURSELF!

One thing I want you to understand is what it comes down to is results, and what type of results are entrepreneurs and business owners looking for? They're looking for more leads, more referrals, and more customers. At the end of the day, that's the bottom line. How can we get more customers so we can grow our business and become more successful, and serve more people? I believe that if you have a great product, you have a great service, you can really benefit others, and you can make a difference in the world. But the only way you're actually going to make that difference is if people buy from you.

So a lot of people have an awesome mindset about selling, and for me, it's your duty — if you truly believe in what it is that you do, and you know what makes a difference — it is your duty to make sure that you serve people so well that they buy. If they don't buy it, they can't leverage it, and they can't make the difference in the world. And for me, in the 15 years that I've been in business, I've realized the number one thing that entrepreneurs specifically are looking for and want as a result is more customers.

That's what every single one of our programs are designed with; obviously, different media and different strategies, but they're all designed to build more trust, more credibility, and positioning you as an expert in your space. Therefore, it makes it easier for people to buy from you, but also refers you to other people who are your perfect customers. In the end, the result is more customers or sales.

In my experience, most of the entrepreneurs that we work with, first of all, are what I refer to as a "Personality-Driven Business." And what I mean by that is they are the face of their business. They are the people who make the majority of the sales and work with the customers and clients, the majority of the time.

I specialize in personal branding because I did it for myself. I have figured out that there was a consistent need and desire among people who are the face of their business and represent their company or their service.

Think of it like this: You might provide one type of service, and I might provide something else, but we're all going through the same exact challenges, and challenge number one is just getting yourself in front of more people. So making more connections, building more relationships. I truly believe, and it's in my logo; it's my slogan. I believe that a business is built on relationships. And actually, in my tagline next to my personal logo, it says: "It's more than business. It's a relationship." Because you're going to connect with people who can potentially become your client or customer or can introduce you to someone that's your perfect customer.

What you want to focus on is building a relationship with them. You don't want to sell to them. And what I mean by that is, if someone connects with you, they feel good about you. If they feel that you're trustworthy, you're credible, and you're an expert, then they're going to realize, "You know what? I'm open to doing business with this person," if they have a need for your product or your service. Now, if they don't have a need for your product or your service, but they know someone that does, because they know and trust you, they're going to be happy to introduce you to that person.

So, the biggest challenge that I've seen for most personality-driven businesses or entrepreneurs is how to connect with more people to build these relationships that will lead to someone saying, "Hey, how can I work with you?" Or, "Hey, can I introduce you to this person?' It really is the number one centerpiece for everyone, and that's why I focused on it personally, building my personal brand, figuring out a way to make faster, better quality relationships with people and being able to leverage the power of branding, marketing, videos, and all of the different collaterals we create.

I let all of those items, together, do the talking for me so that the person sees the value, sees the credibility, and then asks me questions. It really is amazing because I'm very confident that all entrepreneurs feel very similar to the way I feel. I don't want to sell anybody. I just want to provide value, and I want to provide an amazing service. Before I figured all this out, I realized that sometimes I was trying to sell, and the reason that I was selling is because I didn't have enough perceived value in everything that I had available for them to see, hear, and read.

The reason why all the branding, marketing videos, copywriting and graphic design services are so valuable is because they do the talking for you. They position you in a way that people who meet you for the first time, will see value in who you are and what you do, and it will make it easier for you to build a relationship with them. They don't know why, but they will feel attracted.

And when this happens, then they're going to ask you questions, and when they ask you questions, you're no longer selling! You're just providing value because they're interested in what you are offering. And that makes a world of difference in this whole selling arena. I believe this is the number one challenge for entrepreneurs: being able to focus on building relationships and not trying to sell people, and this is very difficult when sales are low or slow.

This is the number one area of focus with our clients at our primary event, which is called *Brand in 2 Days* because it's all based around building the foundation of someone's personal brand. The first thing that we teach and focus on is mindset. Shifting the person's mindset from, "I'm going to this event," or "I'm going to meet with these people so I can try to make a sale" and even though that is true, and that's still going to be happening, and it's still present for me, that's not the question, or that's not the statement I tell myself. I say, "Number one, I'm going to make X amount of relationships tonight, and I'm going to provide value to every single person that I meet," and I already know that, because I have this strategy, this entire marketing action plan.

I don't need to try to sell myself because I have an ace in my pocket. I have my branding; I have my marketing; I have my videos; and I have a process that I already know that I'm going to put these people through so that they can start to build that trust, that credibility, and that relationship. I slow down the sales process so that we can build a relationship first, which will more likely get them to either want to do business with me (because they know me, like me, and trust me) or they're going to introduce me to someone that they know who would be my perfect customer. But understanding that slowing the sales process down, focusing on building relationships, but most importantly, having the right marketing strategy and physical tools that are going to give you that result, is where the magic happens.

I can explain to you in detail how to build a relationship. The problem is this: You can't physically achieve that or effectively achieve that just by you trying to talk to someone. The reason is, if you are having to talk about your credibility, you're losing credibility. And I'm going to say that one more time: If you have to talk about your credibility, you actually lose credibility! So, in my experience, I have not found a way to build a really great relationship with someone so that they feel that I'm very trustworthy and very credible with only me speaking to them.

What has made the biggest difference is seeing visually my graphic design, my branding, reading, which is the copywriting, which is the most valuable tool in marketing—the language, the written word—and watching my videos. The combination of those three elements put together in this Marketing Action Plan, elevates my credibility, my trust, my authority in a way that has never been seen before, which makes them be attracted to me, and then I don't have to sell. I just have to answer questions and give value. And this is the biggest piece of the puzzle that I would say 95% of entrepreneurs are missing.

Not focusing on your personal brand doesn't mean you're not going to get sales, it just means you're not going to get as many sales as you'd like, and you're just going to have to do a lot more work to produce the same amount of results. My favorite thing to tell entrepreneurs is that I create systems and processes so that I can produce more results in less time.

So I actually will go to an event, and I will probably be one of the highest result-producing individuals in that event because of the system I have in place. Not because I'm special, not because I have a better product, it's just because of my system, and anyone could implement the system and the business.

And that's literally what we are teaching. That's what we're creating in the Entrepreneurs Agency, and the one thing that I'd like to share is a realization that I had about *Cracking The Celebrity Code* which is the title of this book. It's really about how to make yourself the celebrity in your space or in your industry, and some people will say, "Well, I don't want to be a celebrity. I don't want to be the face of the business." There's no problem. You don't have to. But if you want to produce more with less work, then this is a bulletproof strategy; as long as you are the face of your business, you are the one that does the sales, and you're the one that works for the customer and the client.

If you sit behind a computer and sell things online, then this strategy most likely will not be as effective for you. And what I realized is this: celebrities are made; they're not born. And the way that celebrities are made is a combination of what people see, hear, and read about these individual people. Now, the key is, it's multiplied by how many exposures they have to what they see, hear, and read about this person.

And I'll give you an example. You hear an artist on the radio for the very first time; you don't know who this artist is. So in your mind, they're not a celebrity. But then you've heard the song maybe four or five times more. They've been interviewed on the radio, you saw them in a magazine article, and then you saw them at the MTV Music Awards. Eventually, they'll elevate to some level of celebrity status in your mind.

The key thing to understand is that it's in your mind; it's a perception. It's not an objective reality. The word celebrity is that we celebrate a person, and we celebrate them because of their successes, right? But the only way to know about the successes is the exposure you have to this person of what you see, hear, and read.

So what I've realized is that this is a formula. It's an actual mathematical formula that can achieve these results in any area. So an individual based on what we create visually, video-wise for auditory and copywriting for the reading. The combination of all these multiplied by creating an omnipresence, meaning getting you everywhere online, on social media, in books, on podcasts, etc. The more exposure we can get to that person within their industry, the more of the perceived value will elevate, and they will become a "celebrity in their space."

That means people will celebrate you, people will be attracted to you, people will become raving fans, and raving fans are the best promoters and best referrers of business in the world. Word of Mouth is still, to this day, the number-one most effective way of advertising. The question is if you don't make yourself something valuable enough for people to be talking about like a celebrity, then it's going to be very difficult for people to be sharing who you are and your message.

I've figured out how to do this. And the best part is I figured out how to do it for myself. As I started to do things in my marketing, in my branding, in my events, when I meet people face to face, I started seeing the results. Eventually, people started asking me, "Rey, could you do this for me?"

And I said, "Yeah, you know what? I could, as long as you are a personality-driven business, just like me, as long as you fit the same criteria as myself, of course." And the reason why all this works is because we're dealing with human beings. This isn't about sales. This isn't even about marketing. This is about relationships with human beings.

And if you really focus on creating this type of relationship and connections and let the marketing and branding do the speaking for you, it just becomes so much easier to do business, and doors that would have never even been a possibility (that you wouldn't even have thought would have been possible) start opening for you. You started getting invited to go speak at places, you get invited to present and to be a part of organizations that you would've never thought because of who you are.

That's really why I'm really focusing on this, "cracking this celebrity code" idea because it makes a tremendous difference. I always tell people, you don't have to agree with me—but trust me, if you try it, you will see the return. Because time is going to continue to go on. Technologies are going to change; we're going to have more and more people out there. And I urge everyone to avoid experiencing what my team I call the "blockbuster effect". The blockbuster effect is when there are new technologies, new opportunities, new information happening around you and you say, "Oh no, that's never going to catch on. I'm the king of this, and I know what I'm doing."

And sure enough, a couple of years later, next thing you know, you're out of business because you didn't stay on top of the trends, new technologies, and everything that's going on. And when I teach people about this celebrity status, what they're not realizing is technology has moved so fast that if they don't start building their brand now and getting themselves out there, soon it's going to be too late. There's going to be people who are dominating the space, so much so, that you won't even be able to catch up. They have hundreds of thousands, if not millions, of followers on Instagram who have a reach extending more than some celebrities do now.

So becoming this celebrity in your industry, I believe, is invaluable nowadays. It's like almost becoming a movie star, and that is going to deliver very high returns, not only for what you do and what you sell but in positioning yourself in a way that's going to attract more business than you've ever thought possible.

"But I Don't Want to Be a Celebrity"

So there's a couple of different examples that I give when entrepreneurs have this concern, and the first one that I give is Tony Robbins. Tony Robbins is the face of his business, but people don't get to work with Tony Robbins directly unless they're paying hundreds of thousands or even millions of dollars. So for those individuals that are concerned about, being the face of their business because one day I'd like to sell my business, or I don't want everyone trying to connect with me.

The reality is it's all about the way that you structure and train your clients as they come on board. As small business owners and entrepreneurs, what usually happens when you're the face of your business, you're the one that's doing everything. So obviously everybody wants you, and they're asking for you even after you start your growth, and you have a team that's taking over the work, they still keep asking for you. But that's only because they've been trained that you are the one that's going to give the results for them.

So, the reality is, making yourself the celebrity in your space will bring you more customers, but you don't have to deal with them as long as you implement the right strategies and educate and train your clients on who's going to service them, how it's going to work, and the flow that they're going to go through.

Tony Robbins will not be working with everybody. And he's built a billion-dollar business at this point, right? So, he's my favorite example for the people that have the concern about, "I don't want to be the face of my business because I want to sell it," or, "I don't want all the work."

For those that are just like shy or don't want to put the spotlight on themselves, here's what I say to that: this isn't about you. Creating yourself to be a celebrity is about serving others. It's not about your ego; it's not about you looking good. This has been a realization that I've discovered over time after doing this because, obviously, I felt uncomfortable in the beginning as well. I realized why it's so important to reach celebrity status: To serve a bigger audience. They'll connect to the celebrity; they'll have an affinity towards a celebrity because they do something for them.

People wouldn't love celebrities if they didn't get some type of benefit from them.

So, the reality is, when you focus on building your personal brand, elevating your celebrity status and putting the spotlight on yourself, the focus is to serve others. It is not about you.

And the moment you shift that mindset and you start realizing, "I'm here to serve others. I'm here to make a difference in the world, and this is one of the best ways to do that because if people don't know who I am, I can't serve them." Then they start to understand, and they start looking at it in a different light. It's not about being the big celebrity on CNN, it's not about that. It's about becoming THE celebrity in your niche.

I always like to use the example of Michael Jordan, because Michael Jordan is a celebrity in sports, and yes, he's recognized all over the world because of being a basketball legend, but if we took Michael Jordan and we put him in ballet, would he still be a celebrity?

Well, here's the question: a lot of the very high-level individual people that are going to see ballet, I would assume the majority of them, especially many of the women, have not been watching basketball, and some women still don't even know who Michael

Jordan is. A lot of people don't know who Tony Robbins is. A lot of people don't know who Les Brown is, who's one of my good friends. And when he was on my talk show, he joked that "I'm known all over the world except right here in Miami where I was born and raised in Liberty City, and people don't even know who Les Brown is."

So we have to understand that we think that everyone knows who Michael Jordan is. We don't realize that there's actually more people in the world who don't know who Michael Jordan is than those that do because it is a perception that we have. This is the key to what I'm trying to get across to entrepreneurs. It's all a perception. It's not actually real. It's just in your mind, and when you have the mindset of "I don't want to be this huge global celebrity," it's not going to be that way. That's just in your mind. And once you shift that mindset and realize that however large of a celebrity you become, you're here to serve and make a difference in the world. Now it's not such a big deal anymore because it's not about you. It's about others.

I will say this, though. Michael Jordan represents Nike's biggest-selling shoe, Air Jordans, Michael Jordan's personalized sportswear. In every speech presentation that I ever made, I put on the slide the Nike swoosh. And I say, "Do you guys recognize this brand?" Everybody says, "Yes," and I say, "Well, the reason you recognize it is because Nike has the most recognized brand logo in the world. That's the Nike swoosh, right?" And I say, "Can anyone guess what's the best-selling Nike of all time?" And everybody will shout out, "The Jordans", "The Air Jordans", and "The Michael Jordans."

And I say, "Nobody said the word 'Nike.'"

And the reason is that the man or the woman will always sell more products or services than the company. And to this day, Nike's top-selling shoes are all sports athletes because people connect with the person. Nike is the most recognized brand in the world, but still, their best-selling shoe has a person's name on it, and the consecutive best-selling shoes also have athletes' names on it.

So I always pose the question, "How does a man's name help sell more shoes?" And the reality is, it's because of the connection that human beings have to someone that provides value or has a very high perceived value. And the moment you implement that into your business, sales will dramatically change. It's not going to happen overnight because you're not going to be a celebrity overnight, but the time's going to pass no matter what you do; this year is going to pass by, regardless.

So, the question I ask you is what are you doing now, today, to start building that celebrity image and status and expertise and trust and credibility for tomorrow, so that in a few years, you are the recognized authority and celebrity in your space?

If you really think about why people are buying, they're buying because of you. And the reason I know that is because you have competition. You're not the only provider of your service or product in the world, and people are still choosing you. The reason they're choosing you is because of the way that they feel about you. Because no one's product or service is so much better than the competition's.

There is nothing out there where the price-point or value proposition is so much greater than the competitor. It's usually within a certain range. And my examples I always give are like Honda and Toyota—which one's better? Then the audience will start giving answers, and I'll say, "You know what? Nissan." And the reality is, Nissan, Honda, Toyota—they're all similar. You can't really say that one is clearly better than the other.

Another example is AT&T vs Sprint: which one's better? I say, "Verizon." Because we really can't specifically say the reasons that we can all agree on which one is better.

So what entrepreneurs are already doing is leveraging the power of who they are. They're just doing it in an inefficient, ineffective way. So they're producing less results than they like.

What's interesting is when I ask clients, "Are you producing the amount of sales that you'd like to produce?" And the answer is usually, 99% of the time, "no." And I say, "Do you feel, based on your experience, your knowledge, your product, your service, the expertise you deliver—do you believe that more people should be enrolling and purchasing your service and purchasing from you?" Most people say "yes."

I teach that one of the biggest factors that is stopping people from making that buying decision is the relationship, the connection, and the feeling they have towards you. And the fact that you might be focusing on selling the product and service as opposed to selling who you are first. Because if you're only focused on the product or service, then you're directly competing with your competitors on their price and their features.

If you focus on building the value in who you are and the way that they feel towards you, now price kind of goes out the window because people are willing to pay more to work and do business with someone that they feel more connected with. They feel that they're going to treat them better, they're going to service them better; they just feel good about it. People like to make buying decisions based on emotion, which is why it's vitally important that they feel good about you.

Obviously, if your products and services are relatively in the same similar price range or has similar features, it can be a little bit more expensive. It could maybe not have one feature or two that the competition has, but if they feel emotionally connected to you, they will choose you. People make buying decisions based on emotion, and back it up with logic.

So I truly believe that if people feel connected to you emotionally, they're going to buy from you as opposed to your competition." I've seen sales increase anywhere between 60% to 70% because of this focus on the emotional connection between human beings as opposed to just the price and the features of the product or service.

Once these concepts are understood, the next step is to do something about it. Well, I hear, "I don't have the time," which we've eliminated because we have a done-for-you, two-day program. So, there goes that one out the window. The other one is, "I'm not technologically savvy." That's the one I do get a lot. "I'm not good with technology."

And the reality is; if you know how to operate your TV and you know how to log into Facebook and turn on your phone, then you can do what we're going to teach you because nothing is that advanced or too technology-driven. Not only that, we're going to teach you everything, step by step. So as long as you're willing to learn the process and do the steps we teach, then you're going to get the results.

This is why I really focused on mindset first because a lot of people stop themselves before they even get started because of the conversation that they have in their own mind. My favorite quote by Henry Ford is, "Whether you think you can or you can't, either way, you're right," and it's one of the things I share with all my clients and we discuss in the beginning because the moment you say that, "I can't do this," or, "It's too hard," well then you're absolutely right.

The moment you shift that and say, "I'm going to learn, and I'm open to following your instructions and implementing what you're teaching me," then you're going to be able to do it. And the only people that have not gotten results from our program are the ones who don't do it, and I think that's obvious. I think we all understand that if you don't do something, you're not going to see the results.

I asked them, "Why are you in business, anyway? Because if you don't want to provide results and make a difference for more people, then go get a job. Because everything that has to do with being an entrepreneur, has to do with your commitment in really impacting the world." And that's also something else that we discuss, and we talk about in our programs; giving back, making a difference, and being a contribution and not focusing on how many sales but how many lives you can impact.

Our experience is that when people amp up their branding and their marketing, people are shocked. They're like, "Wow." They're like, "I know you. I've seen you," and all of a sudden, you're like this new person. And they're like, "Oh, my God, what's going on?" And then they get a lot of praise. They get a lot of congratulations. That's probably one of the biggest, fastest results that our clients see. Even though your friends, family, and people you know congratulate seeing you and giving you praise doesn't actually produce any revenue, it lets you know that you're on the right track. It lets you know that you're doing things in the world, people are noticing; and sometimes, that's all that we need. We just need to know that people are noticing.

But we also have to give them something to notice, right? And that's really why, with the branding, marketing, all the visuals; what you see, what you hear, and what you read, is so valuable. Because if the world is not seeing, hearing, and reading about what we're doing, then how is anyone going to find out, and how are you going to increase sales and build your business if nobody knows about it?

It's like having the Ferrari parked in the garage, but not driving it or telling anyone you have it; so it's kind of counterintuitive if you really think about it.

"I want to grow my business. I want to get my product and service out into the world. I want to make an impact. I want to help more people, but I'm not going to focus on the number one salesperson, which is myself. I'm not going to put the spotlight on me so more people can know, like, and trust me and connect with me so I can serve them." It's almost counterintuitive when you really, really break it down and understand how it's working and say, "I don't want to do this."

That is the reason why you're not producing the number of sales that you'd like to produce is because you do not want to do what it takes to make it a reality.

I ask all my clients when we first get started what their goals are, what they're looking to achieve. Because I won't enroll anyone into our program, even if they're willing to pay for it, unless I know that we can produce the results that they're looking to achieve. One of the questions that I ask is, "Do you want to increase your prices and get paid more for what you do?" And that definitely happens when your brand looks like a rock star celebrity brand.

One of the number-one benefits that our clients experience is they get to increase their prices, and they get paid more for what they do because their value has increased. I have done that for myself personally, year after year after year, consistently, I have increased my prices. Nobody bats an eye. On the contrary, some people tell me I'm charging too little compared to what I'm delivering. Believe it or not, I've consistently doubled my prices over the last several years.

That's kind of crazy when you think about it, because one of the things I talk about is: if you've maxed out all the hours in the day that you can work, for the number of customers you can service, how do you make more money? Then some people will say, "Oh, well, then you have to hire more people." And that's true. But then it costs more, and sometimes once you get to that level, it actually puts you into a deficit.

There are some companies that have a threshold that once they surpass that threshold, it actually costs them more to produce than it does in profits. This is because of overhead. It's just the cost of doing it all. When you've maxed out your hours and you can't service any more clients, the answer is simple: raise your prices.

And like I said, some people might say, "Well, I can't really change my product or my service." But you can change yourself. You can change the value of who you are. That's why the heart surgeon gets paid the most. Right? He's not doing a knee on Tuesday, an elbow on Wednesday, and then work on the heart on Friday. He's a heart surgeon. He's a specialist. He is the celebrity in that space. He is the best at that.

So once you start creating this expertise and this trust and credibility around an area, you can start charging more because of who you are. And some people might say, "Yeah, but I don't sell a service. I sell a product, and I am the face of my business to sell many products."

This is a valid point, but once you build your personal brand and you've created that celebrity status, even though you're selling a product, you can include or add something that has to do with yourself or a service that you provide with your product so that you can charge more. This is my example. I have a SaaS company. I have a software company; it's called My360Sites, and it basically connects all of your digital media in one place at one time, whether it be your websites, your social media, your videos, anything that you may have in the world that's digital and online. This connects it all in one place. What I have is three membership options that you pay monthly, or you pay for the year and you have the service. So, that's it. My prices are set. So how can I increase my price?

I have created a training course that teaches you how to more effectively use the software to get more leads, more customers, and close more sales. And now I sell that course for $1,500, which actually makes me more money than the software itself, but people really want to have the results of getting more customers and more clients. So, they'll buy the software, and then we offer them the opportunity to learn how to more effectively use it by my hands-on, four weeks training course, which they buy because they want the results of fully leveraging the software.

So now, I'm making a lot more revenue with the same product and service that I could not charge more for, but because I've added something, because of who I am, they know that I am a results-producer,

I am great at marketing and sales, and they want my training course.

But if I was just some regular guy and did not have that positioning of a brand of authority, trust, credibility, and expertise, it would be a lot more difficult for me to create that course, sell it to people and have them want to buy it.

Ensuring Success

Well, in our particular case for our clients, we give them the opportunity to come back to our event and refresh the information. So whether it's our event or something else, I'm always going to say that you want to continue to learn, continue to grow as an entrepreneur. It never ends. You're never going to know it all.

So refreshing, even the exact same information when you are at a different place in your life, and your business will absorb differently for you. Actually, I just personally did this myself; I just came back from a retreat. I was in Colorado; I already attended this retreat three months ago for the first time. This was my second time attending.

The reason I do that is because even though it's the same exact information, I'm not in the same place in my business I was three months ago. So, the way I absorb the information and the little tidbits that I picked up were different, and I was able to create something new for my business, out of the exact same event, because I'm in a different place. So, I highly encourage people to come and listen to the information again because new ideas, new motivation, and new connections will be sparked every single time.

I really believe that we should all as entrepreneurs have a mentor that's already accomplished at what we're looking to accomplish, and we want to be a part of a mastermind of like-minded individuals that are going on the same track, who are looking to hit the same goals. We don't have to be in the same industry per se. We just have to be heading in the same direction and looking to achieve the same results. Therefore, we can support one another. There is a lot that is happening in this universe that's not physical, that makes a huge difference in achieving success in life and in business.

I believe once you get around like-minded individuals and voice what you're looking to achieve and commit and get ideas, you're putting that out into the Universe, and the Universe can give it back to you. And the Universe does it whether you call it God or a law or whatever, it's abundant, and there is no limit, and it can give you everything that you want as long as you're open, and you're doing things to be able to put that out into the world so it can feed back to you.

So, I truly believe having a mentor and being part of a mastermind are also things that entrepreneurs should be doing to really take their business to the next level.

NAPOLEON HILL'S MASTERMIND

One of the fundamental factors that we teach in our programs and with anyone that I ever coach or consult with is a principle I discovered for myself; your mindset is key. Your mind is the most powerful muscle and valuable asset that you have to get you to anywhere that you want in your life and in your business.

The reality is, being able to have the proper information and resources to align your mindset in a way that it's going to deliver for you the most doesn't just come from reading books. Reading books can give you a great direction, but I believe that actual action is what really makes the biggest sparks and creates the biggest results.

So, like in Napoleon Hill's *Think and Grow Rich,* he talks about the power of the Master Mind and coming together, you can understand that this is what is going to create success, but you have to go do it. And once you're doing it, that's going to be putting out, like I said earlier, into the Universe, your intentions, your purpose, your direction, and then it gets fired back at you.

And it's really amazing how this all comes together, and really what it comes down to, I believe, is faith. When you believe in something that you can't see, that's not there, but you know in your mind and in your heart that you're going to accomplish it; or that this is what we're after, and then the Universe starts rearranging itself for you to be able to accomplish that.

And it's funny because I've done this multiple times in my life. I can give you several examples and stories of how I've done it, but it all comes down to that I believe that being around others can give you the direction, can give you the shortcuts and can tell you what not to do to not waste your time or your money.

That's really what we've created within our programs is, I've spent hundreds of thousands of dollars, not only in my own education, but in creating the product, services, and marketing content that I now currently use today for myself, but we also provide for our clients. What most people don't realize is you're not just buying this product or the service or this strategy, you're buying a shortcut to not having to go through the mistakes that I went through, not having to spend the money trying to figure it out and spend the time.

So yes, you're buying branding. Yes, you're buying videos. Yes, you're buying a marketing strategy, but you're really purchasing a shortcut to save you time and money and to expedite the growth of your business. And that, I have learned, is the best investment that you could ever make. There is nothing more valuable than that.

I've discovered, and you might've heard this before, "thoughts equal beliefs". Beliefs equal actions, and actions equal results. And I can break that down for you. What we think about consistently, and even what we talk about, our thoughts with others, we will start to believe. Whether that be good or bad, doesn't make a difference. And once we start to believe something, we will start operating.

We'll start acting and doing things in accordance to those beliefs, whether they're good or bad. So if you have a good belief, which is in the direction that you want to take your life and your business, then you will start doing actions in alignment with that, that will eventually deliver the results that you're after. But if you're thinking about things that you don't want, then you're going to believe that you're not going to get them. Which means you'll start operating and doing actions in alignment that will not give you the results that you want because you're focused on what you don't want.

There's a great book, and they made it into a movie called *The Secret*. It was in 2006, that I watched this for the first time, and I was just blown away. I said, "Oh my God, this is what I've been doing all my life and had no idea what I was doing." I was just doing it by default, I don't want to say accident, but I just realized certain things, and I was just doing them.

But when I watched *The Secret*, it actually explained to me what I was doing, which gave me more power because now I understood and I could be intentional about what I was doing, not just doing it by default. And I will say that this is the most powerful thing that I've ever experienced, and still, to this day, use it, and I know so many individuals that do the same.

What's so interesting is that almost 15 years later, I now have not only met, spoken on stage with, but have personal relationships and have their phone numbers and contacts in my phone for people that were in that movie, *The Secret*. Five of them—Jack Canfield, Bob Proctor, Loral Langemeier, Joe Vitale, and Dr. Bob Doyle. I remember thinking that I want to be these people; I want to meet these people. And now I've met five of those people and have their contact information, and I do business with them now, too. So it wasn't just like I went to an event, I met them, and I took a picture. I physically have their contact information, and we do business together.

Some of them have been on my talk show, *Today's Premier Experts*, and I watched them in 2006 when I was just, you know, young in my twenties, learning about this power of *The Secret*. So that just goes to show you, you know, that anything in life is possible, and it's amazing just being able to remember that formula. Thoughts equal beliefs, beliefs equal actions, and actions equal results.

A Marketing Action Plan

We literally created a 15-step Marketing Action Plan that we provide. So, not only do we create everything, not only do we explain to you why it's important and how you're going to use it, but we also give you step-by-step examples and techniques and scripts that I personally use on a daily basis. We literally give you the language and show you how to use it in different scenarios.

We scripted out scenarios for every situation. For example: live events, when you meet someone one-on-one; if you're a speaker and you speak from the stage; if you are on social media; if you're on a podcast; if you're on a radio show; if you're on a talk show; if you're using text messaging. All these different scenarios that we would be connecting with people, and where we are building relationships.

We have a script; we have a process; we have marketing collateral that would be integrated. And my favorite one is our introduction process. It's for referrals, and I teach my attendees that we do not use the word "referrals." We use "introductions" because introductions equal relationship. Referrals equal sales, and I don't want anyone to feel that I'm going to sell to their people, or I want sales. I want more relationships because I know that these relationships through our marketing action plan will turn into a business, which will turn to sales, whether it be directly or indirectly.

We have a step-by-step process, not only with scripting, but with countless digital tools. For example we have something called a "Credibility Card." We teach you how to leverage your story, so that it educates your audience and elevates your credibility (thus the name). We train you on how to do a three-way group text, and how to get these introductions and then move the person from the introduction phase, to a relationship, and inevitably, on your calendar.

Let them research you online through one of our technologies, the 360 site, and then actually have a call. That call will either turn them into a customer or it will have them introducing you to someone who's going to become your perfect customer. Through that entire method and sequence, we teach in multiple different media inside of the Marketing Action Plan.

It delivers results, and you'll see it happen. As long as you follow it and you use it, you will continuously see results every day.

For anyone that is a speaker, this is probably the most valuable investment they will ever make. Hands down; no questions asked. Because as a speaker, obviously, you are the face of your business. You're the number one. You are the celebrity, and you go on stage. So technically, you are a type of celebrity. Enhancing that, creating that connection and getting that out into the world faster and more effectively is the only thing a speaker could ever ask for.

THE BIGGEST BENEFIT

One of the benefits is being able to capture leads from the stage. We've created an amazing system to capture people's information but in a very non-salesy, non-marketing fashion. The focus is on being very relationship-driven. On top of gathering contact details, we allow you to cross-promote yourself through different media platforms—like Facebook, Instagram, and LinkedIn—which will enable you to increase your connections further.

What many speakers don't realize is that it's not just about the sales that you make when you're on stage or the impact you make while you're there. It's about learning how to create a ripple effect and gain more raving fans with each presentation you do. And the best way to do that is to have them connect with you on social media so that you can stay active, in their view, and at the top of their mind. Eventually, this strategy will have them either become your client or one day introduce you to someone whom they know will be your perfect client. This technique for speakers delivers valuable high returns on the back-end, which up until today, most speakers have not been very well-versed or successful in achieving.

This strategy has been huge for me, and I know many speakers who thanked me for teaching them about it as well. Their numbers have increased dramatically from what they were capturing before, anywhere from 20–70% lead capture in the room. I had one client that had 85% lead capture from the room! I've done 100% in small groups of about 15 or 20 people. 100% of them gave me their information because of our system and our process.

While this is amazing, what we provide our clients isn't just a way to capture leads. We also give a whole scripting process on how to follow up with the leads. First, you connect with them, then you build the relationship, get their information, and finally, you have an entire sequence to follow up with them via text message, which is the most effective approach. With text messages, there is a 92% open rate as opposed to 7% on email or 2-7% on mail.

This system has worked out well for our clients because now they're getting calls scheduled after the event. It could be a week, two weeks, or two months later because of the text messaging follow-up campaign, and they don't have to do any of the work.

That's been phenomenal for our clients who are out there, continually speaking and connecting with people. Most of those leads are falling through the cracks because they don't have a great system, and we help solve this!

Case Study Example

At our last branding event we had someone that is in the home servicing business; he has a family business and does plumbing and HVAC.

He also wants to get into speaking to help get the word out about the business. There is a transition in any company based on how you position yourself. So, he came to Brand in 2 Days with his wife, and we did their branding for them and their company. The focus was not just on their company as a family and a team, but we built his personal brand as well. Now he's leveraging it to get speaking engagements at trade shows and events that have to do with his industry. This is the power of expanding your brand!

And now that he's becoming a thought leader, he's no longer just an owner of a plumbing and home servicing business. He's becoming a celebrity in his space. His market is starting to view him in a higher position. He's going to write a book, and he's going to start creating a program on how to teach other business owners who own plumbing and HVAC businesses, how to run their businesses more effectively. This creates a new revenue stream by teaching others how to do what he's doing. Effectively, he's turning potential competitors into clients!

Mindset is Critical

We've discovered that it's so rewarding to see someone who never thought that this was even a possibility in their space, in their industry, to experience a new level of success. What makes the most significant difference is how they feel. They might be doing well or making money in their business, but it might not be something that they're very passionate about, or they might not be making that much of an impact in the world.

So once you start focusing on building your personal brand and who you are, you can make more of a difference, and that fulfills you inside out, which is so much more valuable. I believe this is what makes you more successful. Ironically what makes you successful is not how much money you make, how you live your life or even how you feel; it's the impact make. It's what you can give back to the world.

Maya Angelou said: "I've learned that people will forget what you said, people will forget what you did, but people will never forget how you made them feel."

This ties into building a relationship. When you can make someone feel that they know, like and trust you, that deepens the relationship, and you will get what you ultimately want. This may be increased business, whether it's from them or from someone that they know. They won't feel pushed to do something with you if it's not a good fit, but they understand and respect you and can introduce you to someone who would be a better fit for you.

This has been one of my biggest golden nuggets that I have experienced. I was recently the keynote speaker at an event called CEO Space, and I was speaking with a professional speaker. I asked her about making sure that she gets as many leads as possible from the audience after her talks. She said that she didn't necessarily want to capture leads from the whole room, but only the people that are interested in her topic.

I explained that I understood where she was coming from and that I used to feel the same way, but in my opinion, you should want to lead-capture the whole room because you want to build a relationship with everyone. You want everyone to know, like, and trust you so that they become a raving fan. And then from there, you can figure out who are the ones that are a good fit and determine if they're interested.

It's incredibly important to understand that you can still focus on those who are not a good fit or are not interested. You can still help them see you as a trustworthy and credible expert. Then they are going to be open to introducing you to someone that they know that's your perfect customer. This becomes an entirely new marketing strategy that most entrepreneurs and business owners are not considering.

Every single person knows at least one person in their database that can be your customer! The question is, how do you position yourself in a way that gets them to make that introduction?

That's where the real magic happens. Because, of course, you can just ask people, "Hey, do you know anybody?" Still, they're not going to be motivated and inspired to make the introduction or even think about the person unless they're feeling a connection with you. You must elevate the perceived value of your personal brand because it is extremely valuable to your business.

When I began doing this in my own business, I discovered that I had so many people introducing me to others which led to more connections, relationships, and clients because of how they felt about me— not because of what I do but because of who I am.

Inspiration to Succeed

I wanted more customers and more business. The catalyst was that I became a speaker. I decided to attend a speaker camp to learn how to be a professional speaker.

Now, I wasn't a professional "paid" speaker where people would hire me to speak at an event and get paid. Even though that happens, I was learning to become a "speak-to-sell" speaker, which means that you share your message, expertise, education, and at the end of your talk, you provide a solution to the problem, and what you educated them on, which is your service. Then people buy; it's selling one to many, as opposed to one-to-one.

So I liked that concept of moving away from all of the one-on-one presentations to discover opportunities where I could speak to an entire audience, and make three, four, five, or ten sales or more in an hour and a half!

I loved that concept, and I started to analyze what all the other professional speakers were doing. And because of my marketing and branding background, I wondered if I could create a system and a process that could be even more effective than what most speakers were doing.

Now I have figured it out!

I feel that I have an unfair advantage because not only am I a decent speaker, but I have so much marketing and branding knowledge that I can do things that the majority of speakers are not even considering. It's not in their wheelhouse. Speaking is what they do, and that's all they focused on. In reality, I'm a speaker second because I'm a marketer, branding expert, and entrepreneur first.

The impetus was a testimonial video, created by my team, from some of our clients for our production company, AMP Productions which I have owned for almost 15 years. When I watched the edited video, I realized that none of my clients were talking about the company—they weren't talking about the business; they weren't talking about the website; they weren't talking about the logo.

They were talking about my team and me!

They spoke about the impact that we made and how we treat them like family and care about their businesses. They commented about how we operate with integrity and the results that we've been able to produce for them. That's when it hit me, until then, I had been so focused on building this company and growing this brand, but no one talked about the company or the brand. All they talked about was my team and me. Then the light bulb went off. I had a divine moment, and I realized that I was the number one salesperson in my business!

To this day, I still am the number one salesperson in my company, even though I brought in some salespeople.

I realized people are buying from me, not because of my company or because of my services. The number one benefit they're receiving has to do with my team and myself. As I was learning to become a speaker, I remember adding my picture and my expert title on all of my company branding. I hadn't changed my logo; I hadn't changed my colors or anything. I just added myself to the branding. As a result, I started seeing better connections, faster relationships. Things started flowing quicker, and I wondered if it was just a coincidence!

Then it got to a point where I saw the difference in marketing myself and not my company. After about three years, I transitioned to the point where I don't even talk about my company anymore. Nobody even knows about AMP Productions until after they start working with me. All they know is who Rey Perez is. And I've gotten to a level now where I even have my own personal logo with my slogan. "It's more than business; it's a relationship." I have my personal website, and when I meet people, I give them only my personal brand. I don't talk about my company anymore. I talk about the results that we produce and sales, and I have doubled my revenue every year since.

Now, I'm Diving Into This as a Mission!

I'm really on a mission to figure out how to squeeze the most juice out of this orange because other people are successfully doing it out in the market, and I see the similarities because I'm doing similar things. One of those people would be Grant Cardone. Another would be Tony Robbins, and another, Gary V.

These gentlemen are using their personal brands to make a lot of money; and I'm watching them make money on things outside of their primary services. They are booked to speak on other stages, making hundreds of thousands of dollars without doing anything related to what their actual business is. It still increases the revenues of their internal business, but they're making revenues outside of it.

This is precisely what I'm doing on a smaller scale because, currently, I'm not investing any money on digital marketing or advertising. This is the most significant selling point about what we do.

If you want to increase your leads, your introductions, and your sales without spending a dime on advertising, then focusing on building your personal brand and having this marketing strategy is the way to go. I know this because I've doubled my business year after year, by leveraging the power of my personal brand (which is really just another way of saying my personal reputation). I've done zero online advertising or marketing. I haven't spent any money. Everything's organic.

I've gotten to a point where now I have enough disposable income that I can invest in online marketing and advertising and try this out. I don't know what the results are going to be because I don't know anything about that space. I do know, though, what my results are when I speak to someone, build a relationship, build a connection, and have a conversation.

Now, for the first time, I've gotten to a point where I'm about to start launching digital marketing campaigns to test how they work. I'm excited to see the results. But I do feel that because I have such excellent groundwork, there's going to be a positive response.

Most people have it backwards. They will launch a digital campaign, but when people see their brand, they don't resonate with it. So when you are doing it right and developing the personal brand the right way, you get the results you want increased business referrals, introductions, and leads.

I've seen so many entrepreneurs and clients of mine go through this process and lose so much money because they did it backwards. It's sad to see because the person who's going to be offering you digital marketing is not going to tell you, "Hey, you shouldn't buy my service right now. You should do this first." Instead, they're going to do their job and say, "Hey, we delivered; you didn't make any money because you didn't convert the leads."

Timeless Lessons Learned

My biggest lesson goes back to when I started my lawn service. I was 14 years old and sold the business at the age of 20 for $25,000. The lesson I learned was to give excellent service, go above and beyond. Don't just provide good service, and don't just do a good job. Go the extra mile. Do the extra work that you're not getting paid for. Always deliver absolute excellence because not only will that give you customer retention, it will also provide you with customer referrals and introductions that will help you grow your business!

The most important thing for an entrepreneur is your reputation. If you have a reputation of excellence and integrity, people can share that with others. It makes it so easy for me to get customers because when someone meets me for the first time, they've always gotten great feedback from my other clients about the work that I do. I've received many speaking opportunities because of that. They even tell me: "Hey, I asked around, and we got great feedback about you, so we'd like to invite you to speak at our event." This has happened multiple times. So, before anything else, make sure that you are always providing excellence and constantly going far and beyond with integrity.

It is Important to Recharge

I have a couple of different things that I do because traveling nonstop is very taxing, and you're giving your all to your audience. Number one, I usually just have a day of rest so I can relax. For example, when I get home from a speaking engagement, I may sleep until late afternoon, lay by the pool with my little dog, relax, and have dinner at home. I spend one entire day just relaxing in order to recharge.

I also love going to the beach. I feel that when you're grounded with the earth, and you can put your feet in the water, you kind of cleanse and refresh yourself. I'm lucky enough that I live in Miami so I can do that year-round. I sometimes go get a massage or go to the spa because you have to take care of yourself, and you have to appreciate yourself in all that you're doing and show yourself some love so that you're able to give that back to other people.

Advice Learned at a Young Age

Whatever you do, always do the best that you can; and then strive to do even a little bit better, no matter how much you're getting paid and even if you're not getting paid!

That's one of the biggest things I can share. Do everything in your life with excellence and always go far and beyond, regardless of if you're getting paid. This mindset has made me successful in everything I've ever done because people will notice. And when they notice, they share that with others, which only improves my brand.

Your Brand Is a Declaration of Your Quality to the World

Brand in 2 Days was created when I figured out all of the components that I had to put together to build my personal brand. Then I formulated a process for clients.

When we first launched, we could deliver everything in 30 days or less, but after about 100 clients, we discovered the reason it took us so long: the clients were busy, and it took time for them to get back to us with an answer or to fill something out. Then I had a realization: if I had their undivided attention for X amount of time, I'd probably get everything done in about two days

A light bulb went off in my brain, and I decided to create a system and a process for everybody working at the same time in the same location. That's how Brand in 2 Days was born. The idea is that we deliver professional copywriting to communicate someone's Expert Title, their Unique Selling Proposition, and their Credibility Bio accurately.

These are the three pieces of content that will be used the most when people meet you for the first time or start to interact to build a relationship with you. Photography is really important, especially a good-looking headshot, and our headshots are a little bit different from most people's headshots because they're not cropped.

So it really gives a little bit more of the person's body on a profile photo. It makes our clients connect with the viewer and see some authority. We also create a graphic design and find the right brand colors that are going to position our client and provide the emotion that they want to evoke in their potential customers or clients.

So a profile image would go on Facebook, LinkedIn, Instagram, YouTube, as well as your email signature, digital business card, physical business card, print banner, social media signs, and all various digital collaterals. We take all the components of the photography, graphic design, copywriting, and we blend them together to create this cohesive, trustworthy, and credible brand. And then we distribute it across all the different channels.

It's our syndication process so that more people can connect with you, and no matter where they land on your brand, they're going to see the same trustworthiness and credibility, not only visually but also in language. From there we have the social media marketing strategy of how to use it along with our Personal Brand Marketing Action Plan, which is a step-by-step checklist on how to use each branding collateral. There are 15 collaterals in total that we create within the two days, along with how to use them effectively, and what script to use as well.

We teach the proper sequencing and timing in the relationship-building process to use it, and how it is to be delivered, whether it's through social media, email, text message, or just simply in person. So all of this is put together works in harmony and we provide this in just two days. Based on feedback and the desire of our clients to jump right in to get things done, we have created an additional event which is the day directly after Brand in 2 Days. It's called the Marketing Implementation Bootcamp.

This event is optional. It is a separate cost, and many of our previous clients choose to come back to this event as well. The whole point of the Marketing Implementation Bootcamp is to go over our Personal Brand Marketing Action Plan and physically work with our attendees to practice using the scripts that we've taught them and the collaterals that we've created for them in Brand in 2 Days.

I had been doing Brand in 2 Days for almost a year and realized a lot of people were not effectively implementing what we taught because obviously, it takes time. It's also a learning curve, and people are busy. So I thought, what if I created a full day dedicated to just working with them and expand on the training on how to use everything we've taught them? The Marketing Implementation Bootcamp has become one of our most popular events for our clients because it delivers the maximum results for them in the shortest amount of time. It's also a great way for our clients to network with some of our returning clients who attended a different Brand in 2 Days.

Frequently Asked Questions About Brand in 2 Days Event

Over the years, we have found that there are several questions that we are asked about our Brand in 2 Days event. These are the ones we hear most often:

"Does my branding need to look like everyone else's? How will I stand out?"

So that's a really good question. That happens occasionally. People see the rest of our clients and that we have a formula to it—that they look similar. Everybody's got a different picture, language, and color, but they look similar because there is a process and a template that we've created for mobile devices and for computers that have proven very successful for us. What we don't want to do is change the template because then it might not deliver the same level of success. If we all drove Lamborghinis with different colors and came in different models, other people are still going to be wildly impressed and they are going to say, "Even though all those are Lamborghinis, they're all beautiful and super fast." Because at the end of the day people mostly care about performance.

It's really about what this is going to do for you. Not necessarily, "Oh, I want mine to look different from everybody else's." It's about what you're going to get out of it. And the reality is the only time that you look like everyone else is when you're parked right next to everybody.

And that actually has happened because I've gotten a lot of speakers that have enrolled in my program and that speak at similar events with others and have been next to each other, and it does look very similar. You can clearly see that they're different brands, but you can tell that they're part of the same community, the same family.

And the way I look at it is, look, you want to be part of the Lamborghini or Ferrari family because when it's all said and done it just shows quality, it shows value. But the moment you leave that event, you will be the only one in your space because that doesn't happen that often.

It happens every once in a while. And really what I encourage people to focus on is the results of the performance of what they're going to get from the brand, not on trying to be unique and individually different.

If we know it works and we know it produces results, why wouldn't we use it? And I know some people are like, "oh, yeah, but I want to look different." Well then, do that, but you just might not get the same results that everybody else is getting. If you go get yourself a different type of car and everyone else's Lamborghini and you're way behind, you know the reason why. So it's kind of a catch-22, but there's a reason, and there's a purpose that everything has the structure so it can deliver the maximum results.

Does everyone have to come to the onsite location in Florida to get all of the branding done?

Technically you don't. We highly recommend you come in person and experience the event live because there's so much that happens here when you're physically involved with something. But we do offer a digital opportunity to attend virtually. So you will physically be in the room with us, but you'll be through a webcam, via Zoom and you'll be listening to everything, experiencing, giving your feedback just as if you were in the room.

It would just be virtually through our online video conferencing platform. And at the end of the day, we still deliver the exact same results. You still get the exact same products. The only difference is that you will be responsible for taking your own headshot photo because you won't physically be with our photographer. And you miss out on the networking opportunities. I can't tell you how many joint ventures started right here at Brand in 2 Days.

What's the investment for the packages?

When you spend money on marketing, as long as there's an ROI; it's an investment. This is truly one of the best investments that any entrepreneur will ever make for their business because it's really an investment in themselves.

And that's the beautiful thing everything we do here. It doesn't matter if you change your business today or have a second business tomorrow. Your personal brand will always live and breathe because it's you, and you will use it for everything, you will use it on a daily basis.

We have a couple of different options because we understand that not every entrepreneur is in the same place in their business financially, length of time, status, as well as other variables. So we've created basically everything I've ever done for myself into one big package, which is about $30,000 and it includes everything.

Then what we did is we chopped up that $30,000 package into a few different options, and we made this 30 step growth track so you can start, come on board and attend Brand in 2 Days as low as $500. Here you will learn all the strategies, the marketing, everything that we teach and not get the physical branding done with us. That's for someone that maybe already has a copywriter, a social media team and graphic designers. In that case, an attendee might say to themselves, "You know what, I can do all this stuff with my team." So if they just want to know the strategy, the process, the methods, and the systems, they can just attend the event as an attendee-ticket only.

We have three branding packages, the biggest one being our $30,000 all-inclusive *Celebrity Icon Branding Package*. Then we have our starter package which is the *Networker* or Branding package; it starts as low as $2,000. Finally, we have our Influencer Branding package, which starts as low as $5,000, and those are the three main packages.

So depending on where people are at in their business, we'll sit down with them, ask them some questions first to really figure out where they want to go, what is the goal, and what are they looking to achieve. And then from there, we will recommend which package is best for them accordingly. And they can always upgrade and move on to the next one as they move forward.

What if I'm not really photogenic, or I want to lose weight?

So when anyone is concerned about their image, I mean obviously our responsibility is to make you look great. So we have a really, really great photographer. He's one of the best headshot photographers in the country who specifically focuses on headshots (a key difference if you're ever looking to get headshots).

So we make everyone look great, and when I tell people this, if you don't like your photo, that's completely fine. We just need to see what everyone else thinks because it's not really up to us.

Remember what I said about the brand; this isn't about us. This is about servicing other people. And it's one of the mindset challenges that we have to overcome with people. To realize, "Okay, I might not love my photo, but everybody else seems to like it and is happy with it." And that's all that matters because we're here to serve others; we're not here to make it about us.

The second thing is if you're looking to lose weight or you're looking to make some changes, our *Influencer Package*, our Branding Package, and our *Celebrity Icon Package* allow you to come back to Brand in 2 Days so you can do exactly that. So nothing's set in stone. You can come back three months, six months, a year, and you can update those images with a new headshot. And even if you want to change some of the colors, the language, you're able to do that as well.

Can I bring a guest?

Yes! We include the opportunity to bring a guest. Whether that's a spouse or someone that works with you (an assistant or business partner). We give you a second ticket which you can actually gift to someone that either you know, who has a business, or is an entrepreneur.

One of the things that we focus on is giving, being in an attitude of gratitude, and our *Influencer Package* is at the core of that. So we want to give you the opportunity to give to someone else, to gift them the attendance tickets to be part of Brand in 2 Days.

Is video included in the branding package?

Our *Celebrity Icon* branding package does include multiple videos as well as being a guest on our talk show, *"Today's Premier Experts,"* which is aired on Amazon Fire, Apple TV, and Roku. We interview celebrities and experts in different niches and industries, and I've had some amazing guests like Les Brown, Kevin Harrington from Shark Tank, and many others. And it's a great platform not only to get your message out to the world, but to also give you more trust, credibility, and eyeballs through all the different channels.

So, all of that is included inside our *Celebrity Icon*. However, during the actual "Brand in 2 Days" event, we allow up to five individuals the opportunity to add additional packages to get video production done. This is not included in either of the first two Brand in 2 Days packages, but they are separate packages depending on the person and what they're trying to achieve.

We have a production studio, and there's only so much time. And the benefit is that you come for two days to get your branding done, and you get a couple of videos done within those same two days. Now, you actually produced even more in the same amount of time. For an entrepreneur, there's nothing more valuable than that.

How quickly are we going to notice a difference? When do I see results?

Well, I love that question because the reality is, you'll start seeing results the moment you put the branding out into the world. And like I said earlier, your friends, your family, people who know you, who have known you for a long time all of a sudden are going to be commenting, and sending you messages, asking you questions and that just lets you realize right away that, "Whoa! This does make a difference. We really are going to get some results."

Because if they know you and they're being impacted, when people who don't know you see it, imagine what that impact's going to be because people are judging based on what they see, what they hear and what they read. So if you are already known as trustworthy and credible, and we've put communicated that to the world, people will start noticing immediately.

My favorite part is when you meet someone for the first time, and you use the steps in the process and use our digital business card and use our 360 site technology, and you notice their reaction right away.

They'll be impressed; they'll be wowed, they'll literally use the word, "*wow*! "

When someone uses that word, when they have any interaction with you, you know you're doing the right thing, you know you're on the right track because it's all about creating a wow experience for people when you meet them. It's the ultimate first impression and we all know you only have one chance at that.

How will I attract more leads and referrals?

Let me explain it this way: I like, very cool exotic cars. I have a green i8. I've had some Ferraris and Lamborghinis and other cool cars.

And I always say, if your friend pulls up in a Lamborghini or a Ferrari, or some exotic car and other people who know you start seeing it, do you think they're going to ask you about that person?

It's just the way humans work. I talk about how I relate to people as cars. We're all different models of cars. The way I explain it is if there was a big parking lot full of cars, all different models, and I'm walking through the parking lot, and I see a Honda or a Toyota, well, I basically just keep walking. If I see a BMW and a Mercedes. I might just take a look at it, but if I see a Bentley or a Ferrari, what do most people do? They stop, they stare—maybe even take a selfie!

So I asked the question, "Why?" Why do we do that as human beings? And the answer is because we're attracted to things that have a higher perceived value. So when someone gets introduced to you for the very first time, whether it be in person, whether it be online, or whether it be through an introduction by text.

When they see you, visually and contextually, with a high perceived value; they're going to be immediately attracted. They don't know why, but they will.

Once you put this branding system in place and you start using it, you will see how people react to you as if you were driving a Ferrari.

What's the biggest benefit that I'm going to see, what are some of the residual benefits?

The biggest benefit I see is that you will start building raving fans, and that's when you start really building this status of who you are. That, in itself, will give you long-term results. Meaning, you're going to now start being introduced to high-level individuals that you might've not been introduced to before. People will start being interested to do joint venture partnerships and work with you who previously didn't even have you on their radar, and all of a sudden, new doors and opportunities start arising not because of what you do, but because of who you are or, more specifically, because of the perception that people have of who you are. That is what makes the biggest difference, that's what delivers the most results, and lives on in the long-term.

How is personal branding tied to return on investment?

You can't put a specific price point, like I got this particular sale because of my personal branding. Your personal branding can affect everything you do. That's the best part. It isn't just one thing. It's not like, "oh, I did this Facebook marketing advertising, and this is what we did from it."

Your personal brand is used everywhere. So it's going to affect everything you do, whether it be in person, whether it be through digital designs, whether it be on social media, whether it be through email—it's all about you. It doesn't matter if it's one business or another, that's the beautiful part. Your personal brand will benefit all that you do in your life and in your business or businesses. That's another benefit of having a strong personal brand, you can leverage your following, no matter what venture you're involved in. You have your primary business, but let's say you want to start another business in a different industry or you want to start a non-profit charity organization; with your personal brand, you can redirect or existing audience that you've built and funnel them to your next venture. But to build that audience you have to shift how they see you and that's made possible with the power of branding.

You can feel the difference when that happens, and that is going to directly affect the results that you achieve and everything that you do. So, it's more intrinsic, but I always tell my clients, "You will feel the difference." When I drive around in my car, in my BMW i8, which is green, and the doors go up. . . I feel a difference from when I drive in my BMW X6, which is still a beautiful car. It's still $80,000, but, at the end of the day, it doesn't have the visual appeal.

And everyone who sits in my car with me and drives around feels the difference. That's the best example that I can give: You and everyone around you will feel the difference when you have this personal brand out in the world.

The reality is this: if you really want to grow your business, if you want to be successful, if you want to make an impact and change in the world and you've realized that you're the one that is making the difference in your business, then I highly recommend that you invest in the most valuable asset that you have, which is yourself. Don't wait, because the longer you wait, the more time is going to pass, and your competition is going to be catching up or passing you. Then it makes it so much more difficult to stay ahead or to even catch up because of time and technology.

This doesn't happen overnight. I didn't get to the level that I am in one year. I can tell you that it was about two and a half years where I really started seeing the fruits of my labor. It got to a point where every time someone would reach out to me, they would say, "Hey look, let's have lunch, or let's have a meeting. I want to discuss doing something with you." The first thing that they would say when we'd sit down is, "I see you're doing great. I've been watching you on social media." And that gave me such validation for what I was doing because they're organically seeing what I'm doing on social media, but they're seeing everything that I've created and am putting on social media, so I know what it is that they're seeing.

I know doors have been opening up because of it. And that I got multiple $100,000 business relationships because of meetings that had to do with someone telling me, "I've been watching you on social media, and I see you're doing great and I want to talk to you about doing X, Y, or Z."

This all started to happen when I implemented my personal brand, and it will for you too!

Implementation Workbook

Now let's put what you've learned into action! Take time now to complete this workbook section with carefully thought-out responses.

This will help you to fully understand your worth in the marketplace and put you on the road to AMP'ing up your personal brand!

Crafting Your Expert Title

1. Think about what it is that you enjoy doing for others and what it is you make a difference doing?

2. What have people said about you? If I ask people about you, what would they say?

3. What kind of results do you like to get?

4. What is your "Elevated Perceived value" – as a human being... That makes people say they want what you have to offer?

____

____

____

____

____

____

____

____

____

____

____

____

____

____

____

____

5. It is all about RELATIONSHIPS... Why do people want to be a part of your tribe? How does it benefit them?

____

____

____

____

____

____

____

____

____

____

____

____

____

____

____

____

6. What are your unique skills or traits?

7. What's is the #1 result that you produce for your clients?

____

____

____

____

____

____

____

____

____

____

____

____

____

____

____

____

____

8. What do you enjoy doing the most?

9. What are you most passionate about?

10. What's your favorite thing about your business?

Made in the USA
Monee, IL
05 May 2021